FOR ORGANS, PIANOS & ELECTRONIC KEYBOARDS

E5

Exploring DOUBLE

C000196559

Double notes is another name for *two-part harmony*. This book shows you how easy it is to play double notes. You'll learn the notes that make up different chords and how to add them to the melodies you play. Once you become familiar with a few basic principles, you'll be surprised at how good you can sound.

Like the other books in the Exploring series, this one cuts through most of the technical material and gets right to the heart of the matter. This allows you to start applying the techniques right away.

Since this book is aimed at electronic keyboards in general, the way some of these techniques work might vary from one instrument to another. It's a good idea to have your owner's manual handy in case you need to refer to it from time to time.

CONTENTS

HAL•LEONARD®
CORPORATION

7777 W. BLUEMOUND RD. P.O. BOX 13819 MILWAUKEE, WI 53213

WHAT ARE DOUBLE NOTES?

Double notes are **two notes that sound at the same time**. The double notes, or harmony, that can be played with a melody generally come from the accompaniment — the chords that your left hand plays while your right hand plays the melody. Here's a well-known example. Press the Voice or Solo button marked PIANO and play CHOPSTICKS with your right hand.

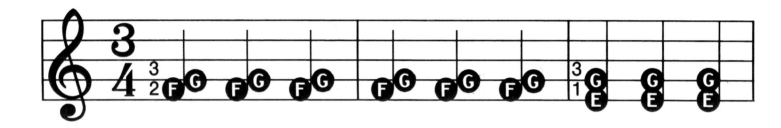

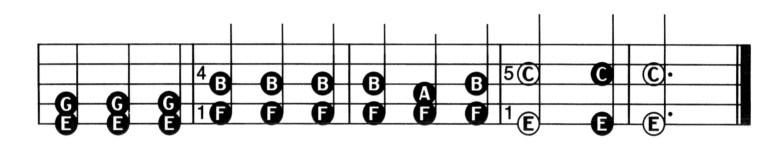

Previously, you might have played this with one finger of each hand; this book will take you well beyond that.

SPECIAL CHORD SYMBOLS

Chord symbols (C F G 7)above the melody tell you which chord to play with your left hand. All of the songs in this book use specially marked chord symbols to help you. Above each chord box are the names of the notes that make up that chord (these are called **chord tones**). They tell you which notes to use for creating the double-note part.

C E G
C

F A C
F

G B D F
G 7

This gives you a choice of two or more notes to use for the harmony, no matter what chord is being played.

In the first songs, the names of the chord tones appear as shown above. After a few songs, when you've become familiar with them, they're shown only on the title page of each song. As new chords occur, they are used within the music until you've worked them into your playing.

INTERVALS

In music, the distance between two notes played at the same time is called an **interval**. Intervals are determined by starting on one note and counting the lines and spaces up or down to the next note.

One interval you might already know is called an **octave**, from a Latin word meaning "eight." If you start on the lower C in the following example, and count the lines and spaces up to the next C, you'll find the count is eight. The other intervals within this octave are also shown. Play and carefully listen to each one.

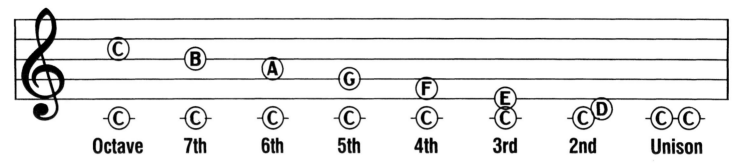

NOTE: The final interval above is called unison (from the Latin **unisonus** meaning "one sound") because there is no distance between the two notes.

The most usable intervals are the 3rd and 6th. They have round, pleasant sounds that fit almost any kind of music. When one of them seems to not work for you, try the other; 3rds and 6ths can be quite interchangeable.

GUIDELINES FOR CREATING DOUBLE NOTES

1. Add harmony only to melody notes that are chord tones (the special chords symbols indicate this).

2. Put the double note **below** the melody note.

3. For now, add double notes only where the melody note is a half note or longer, or where melody notes repeat in the same measure.

4. Try to use the chord tone that lies closest below the melody (remember: 3rds are easiest and they sound good).

Point 4 is illustrated below.

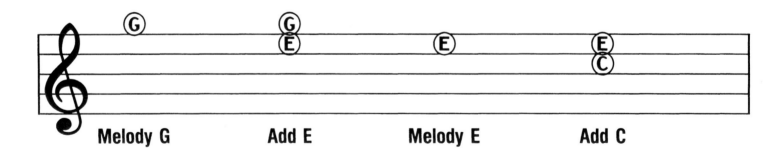

Here is LARGO. Play the melody and chord accompaniment, without rhythm, for familiarization.
Then play the arrangement with the harmony added — and listen.

There is a Registration Guide on page 48 that coordinates with the Registration numbers found on each song.

Largo

Registration 1
Rhythm: Off

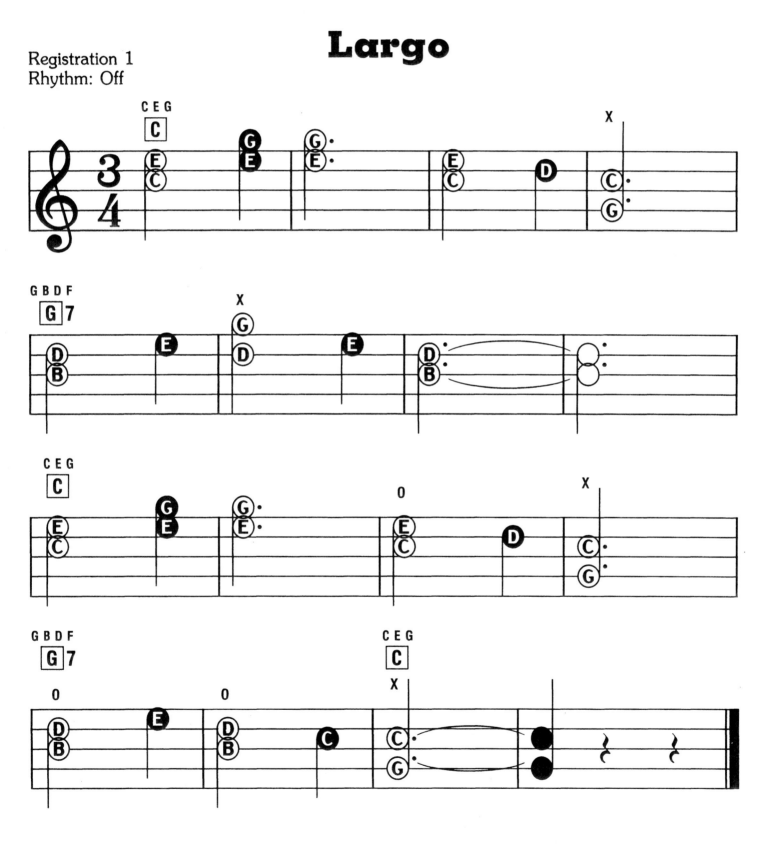

Although we followed the guidelines, a few of the double-note combinations create an open, hollow sound (4ths); these are marked with an X. Here's another guideline:

To change the sound, skip the chord tone directly below the melody note and use the next lower chord tone.

Here are the last two lines of LARGO using the new guideline.

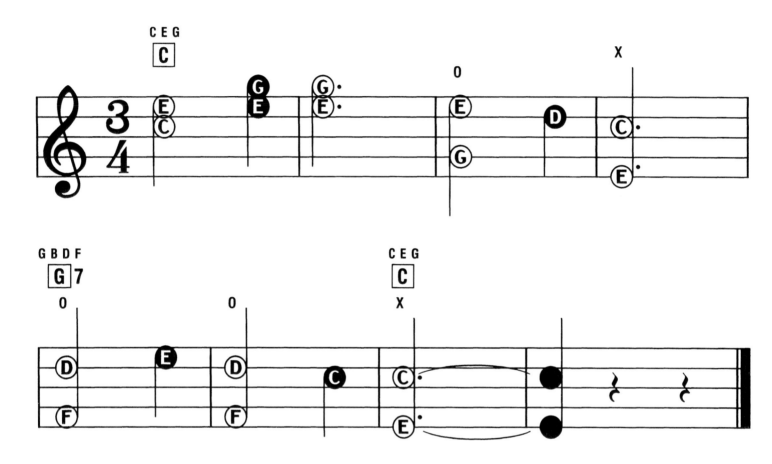

There's a hint in the above examples: If the melody note is the note that names the chord (e.g. melody note C in a C chord), you'll generally get a better double-note sound by skipping to the next lower chord tone. Where the circles appear, we skipped to the next lower chord tone to set up the necessary lower double notes in each of the following measures. This is purely a matter of choice.

Try your hand at it on KUMBAYA on the next page. Be sure to observe the guidelines.

Kumbaya

Registration 2
Rhythm: Rock or 8 Beat

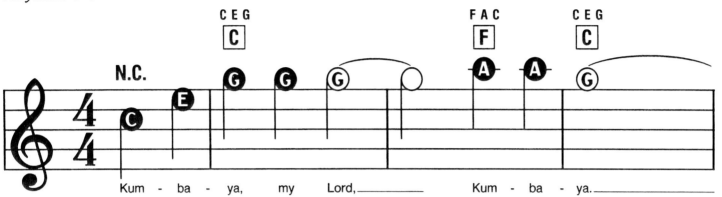

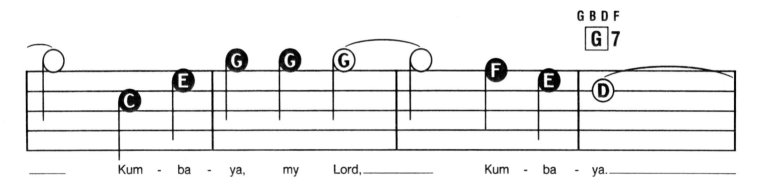

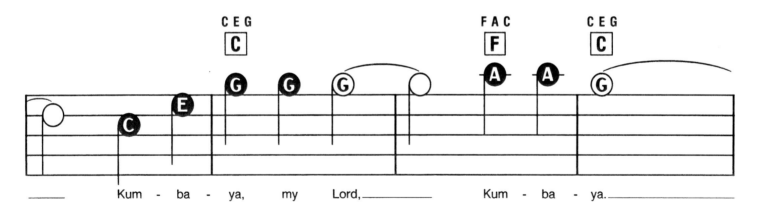

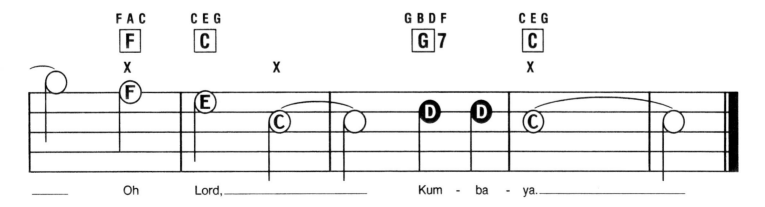

NON-CHORD TONES

Quite often, the melody note you play is not a part of the chord that accompanies that melody note. For example, if you are playing a G in the melody and the chord is F (F-A-C), the G is a **non-chord tone**.

The first step in harmonizing non-chord tones is to identify them. In the following example, from The Everly Brothers' LET IT BE ME, each non-chord tone is marked with an X.

Let It Be Me
(Je T'appartiens)

English Words by Mann Curtis
French Words by Pierre DeLanoe
Music by Gilbert Becaud

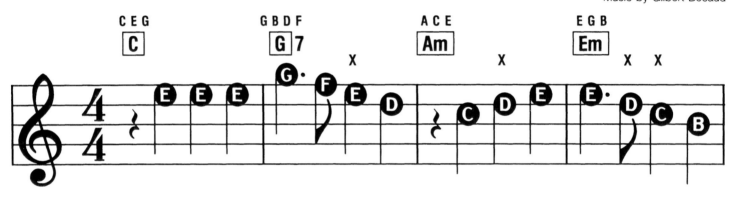

The non-chord tones in the above melody can be called **passing tones** because they "pass" from one chord tone to another, usually in stepwise fashion (line-space-line-etc.). Passing tones are generally a quarter note long or shorter.

A non-chord tone can be harmonized with a chord tone or another non-chord tone. The next section tells how to do it.

THE 3/6 PRINCIPLE

You read earlier that 3rds and 6ths are the basis for playing double notes. We made up the 3/6 Principle to help you create good-sounding intervals, especially in harmonizing non-chord tones. Here it is.

Starting on the melody note, count down the lines and spaces to "3." Play the resulting note along with the melody note and the accompaniment chord.

Does the interval sound good? Does the harmony fit with the harmony note just before and just after it? If the answer to either of these questions is no, start on the melody note and count down to "6" and try again.

Let's apply the prinicple to LET IT BE ME, first using 3rds in as many places as possible.

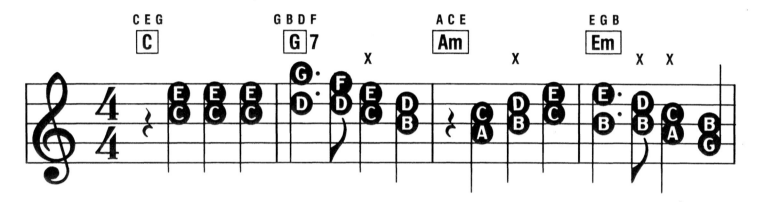

You might like that well enough; however, compare it to the following version which is based on 6ths.

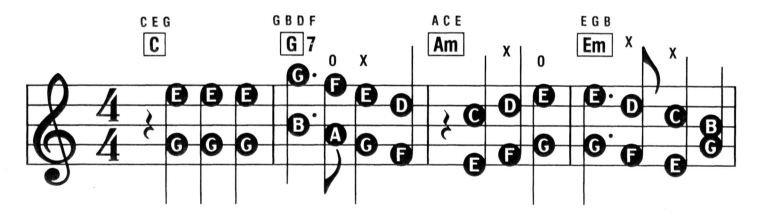

In this case, some melody notes that are chord tones were harmonized with non-chord tones. They're marked with a circle.

While the 3/6 Principle doesn't work every time, try it whenever you need help in creating double notes. Keep in mind that it can also be applied to chord tones as well as non-chord tones.

Let It Be Me
(Je T'appartiens)

English Words by Mann Curtis
French Words by Pierre DeLanoe
Music by Gilbert Becaud

Registration 8
Rhythm: Rock or 8 Beat

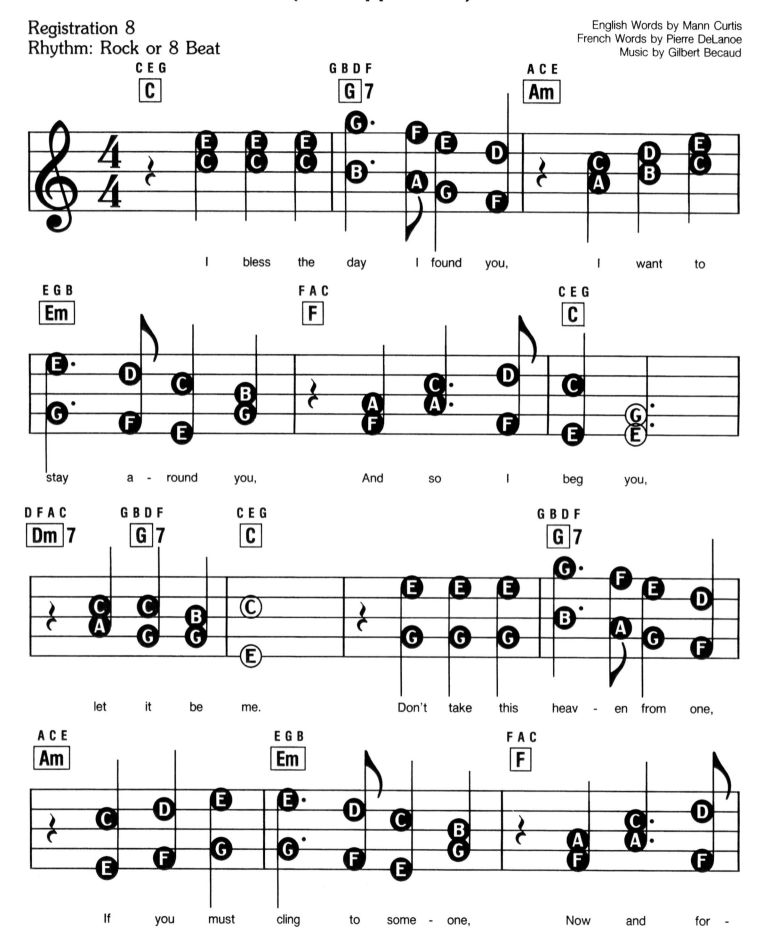

11

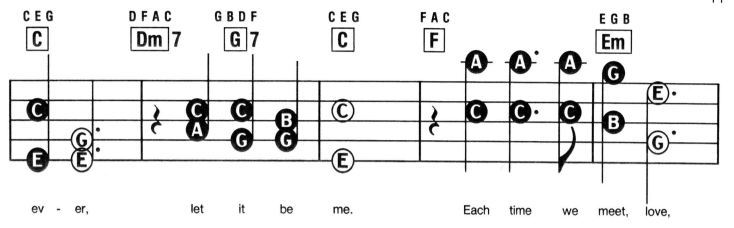

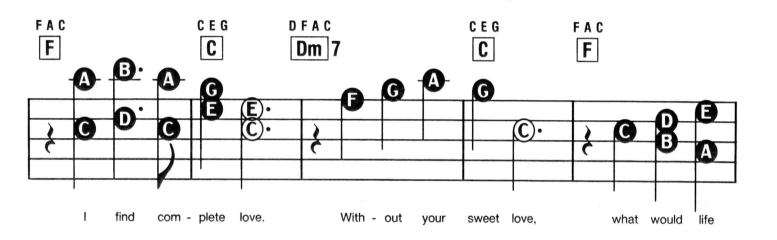

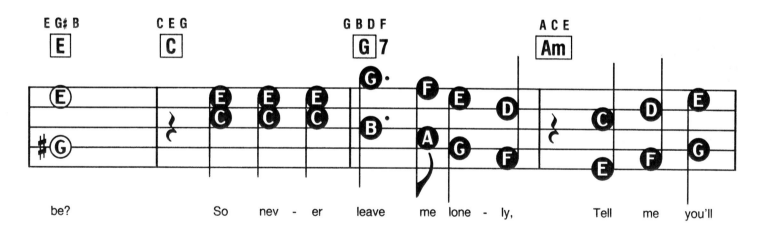

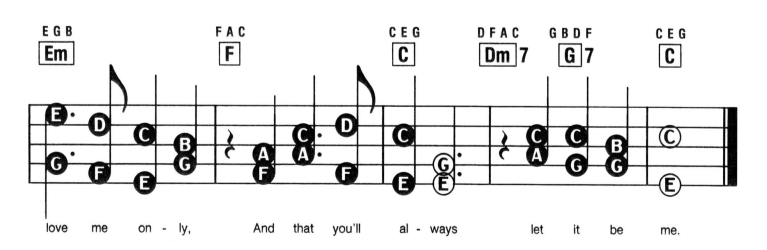

Part of BRAHMS' LULLABY is next. Mark the non-chord tones with an X above each of the notes. Then play the example and apply double notes to everything except the eighth notes. One double note appears in measure 4 as a helpful hint. When you arrive at a harmony part you like, pencil in the double notes below the melody.

Brahms' Lullaby

Registration 7
Rhythm: Waltz

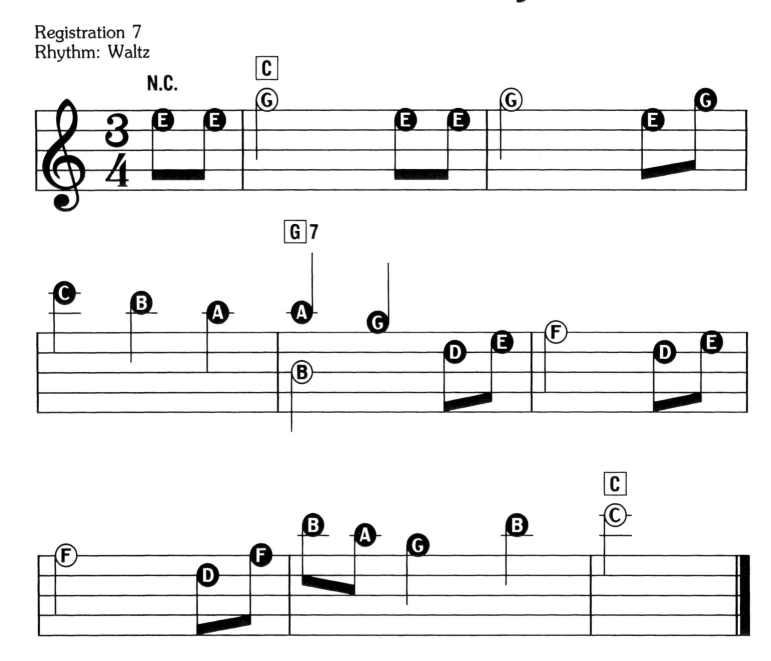

PARALLEL DOUBLE NOTES

Some melodies, or parts of melodies, are such that they allow you to play parallel double notes; that is, the harmony follows the melody totally in 3rds or 6ths regardless of what tones are in the accompaniment chords. Here's an example from the Latin-flavored song, YOURS, which is unusual in that 3rds can be played throughout most of the arrangement.

Yours

Words by Albert Gamse and Jack Sherr
Music by Gonzalo Roig

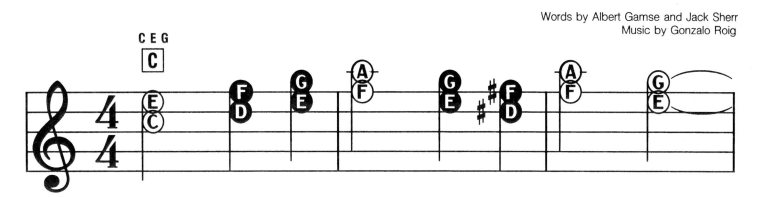

The F♯ in the melody introduces a non-chord tone which can be called a **neighboring tone**. Such non-chord tones are generally just above or, as in this case, below a chord tone (G). Like passing tones, they are usually no longer than a quarter note. As often as not, the double note can also be a neighboring tone; this adds to the effect of parallel motion.

In the third measure, the A is a non-chord tone, as is the F that harmonizes it. Both, however, move down to chord tones (G and E) on the third beat of that measure. The alternatives would be to use an E below the A (creating an interval of a 4th until the G in the melody), or to use a C below the A. You'll likely agree that the parallel 3rds sound just fine.

Play the complete arrangement of YOURS on the next page and listen to the effect of the parallel motion.

A♭C#E G	C E G	D F A	F A♭ C	G B D F
A7	**C**	**Dm**	**Fm**	**G**7

Yours

Registration 4
Rhythm: Rumba or Latin

Words by Albert Gamse and Jack Sherr
Music by Gonzalo Roig

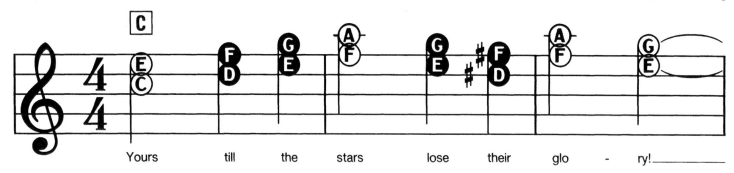

Yours till the stars lose their glo - ry!

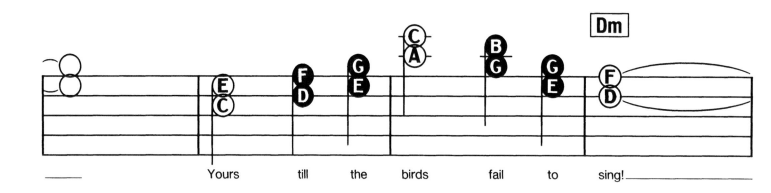

Yours till the birds fail to sing!

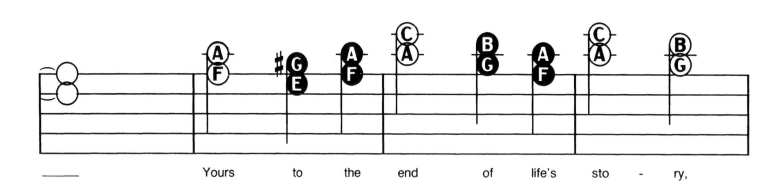

Yours to the end of life's sto - ry,

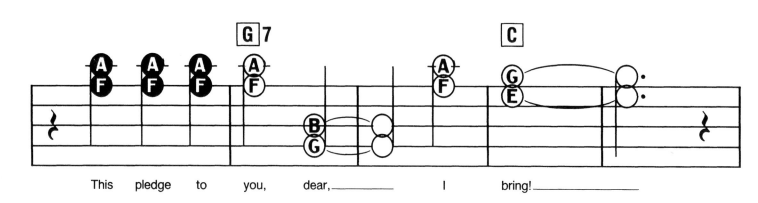

This pledge to you, dear, I bring!

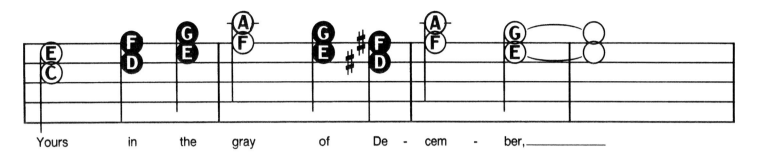

Yours in the gray of De - cem - ber,_____

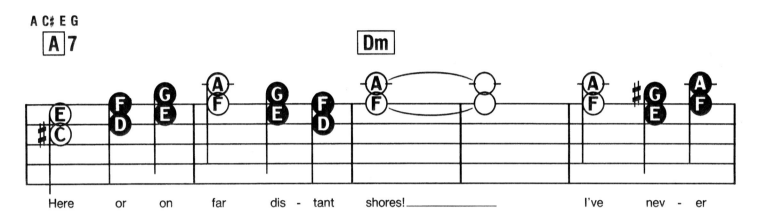

Here or on far dis - tant shores!_____ I've nev - er

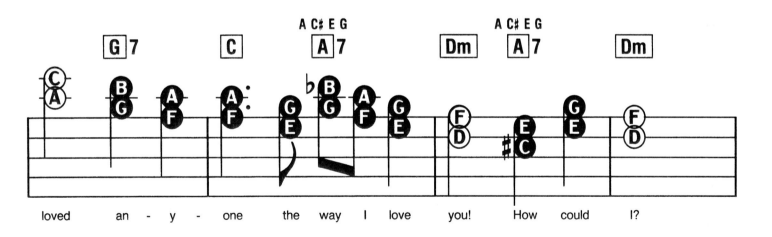

loved an - y - one the way I love you! How could I?

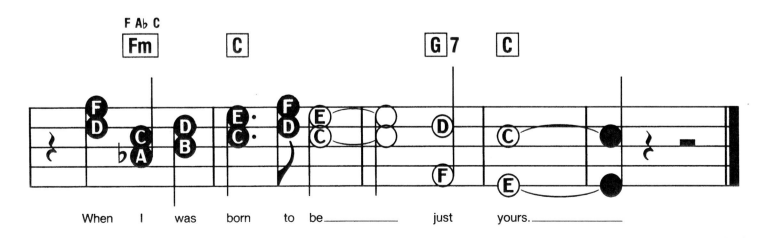

When I was born to be_____ just yours._____

For the record, it's also possible to play some songs entirely in parallel 6ths; it depends on how the melody is structured in relation to the accompaniment chords. Always try both 3rds and 6ths to see if one or the other will work.

A NOTE ABOUT ENDINGS

One place where you should not use non-chord tones is at the end of a song. The best interval is a 6th for two reasons. First, remember that most songs end on the note that names the chord. Therefore, if you're playing parallel 3rds, the double note below the last melody note will not be a chord tone. The second reason is that the next chord tone below the melody note creates the interval of a 4th. Skipping to the second chord tone below provides a 6th. This is why YOURS ends the way it does. It will be helpful if you keep this in mind as you go.

SPECIAL NOTE

Because of the difference in the number of keys from one keyboard model to another, you might find it necessary to play some songs an octave higher or lower than they are written, especially if you are using 6ths (which cover a larger area of the keyboard).

BEAUTIFUL BROWN EYES gives you the opportunity to play double notes in parallel 6ths.

After that, create double notes for DON'T CRY FOR ME ARGENTINA and see if parallel harmony can be used. If necessary, play the song an octave higher than written.

Beautiful Brown Eyes

Registration 4
Rhythm: Waltz

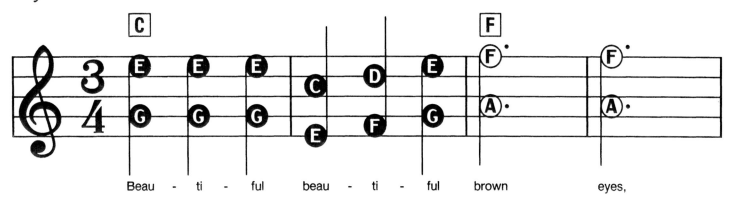

Beau - ti - ful beau - ti - ful brown eyes,

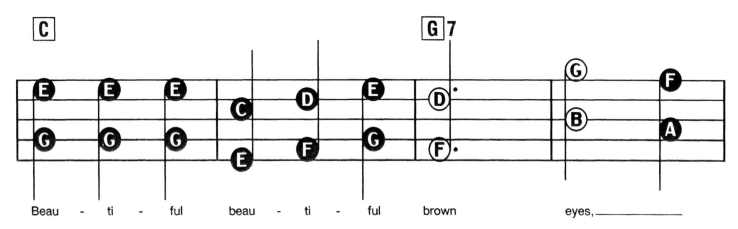

Beau - ti - ful beau - ti - ful brown eyes,____

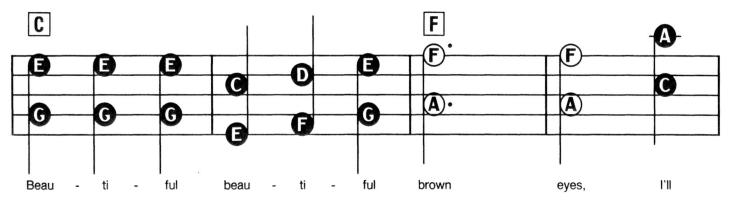

Beau - ti - ful beau - ti - ful brown eyes, I'll

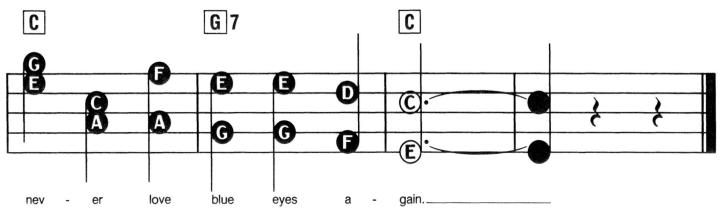

nev - er love blue eyes a - gain.____

Don't Cry For Me Argentina

(From the Opera "EVITA")

Registration 9
Rhythm: Tango or Latin

Lyric by Tim Rice
Music by Andrew Lloyd Webber

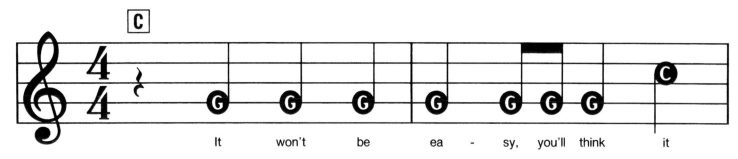

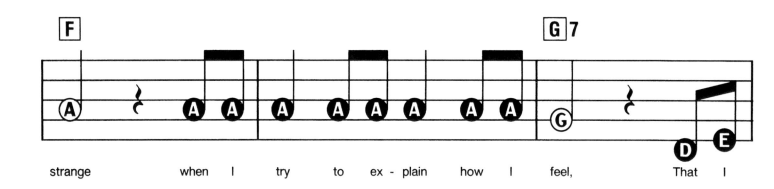

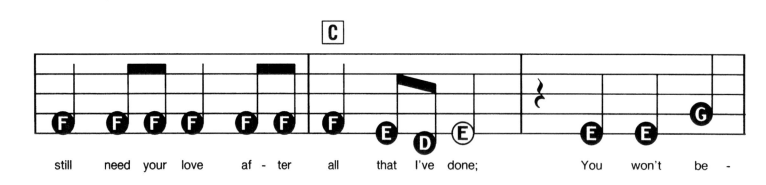

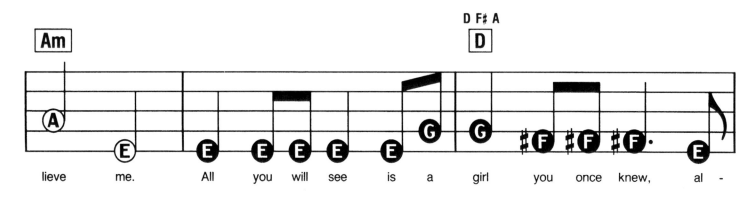

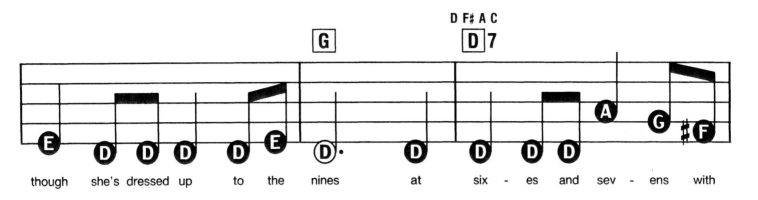

though she's dressed up to the nines at six - es and sev - ens with

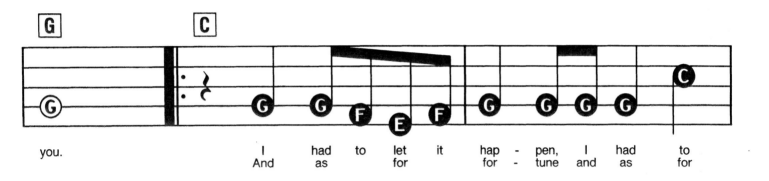

you. I had to let it hap - pen, I had to
And as for for - tune and as to for

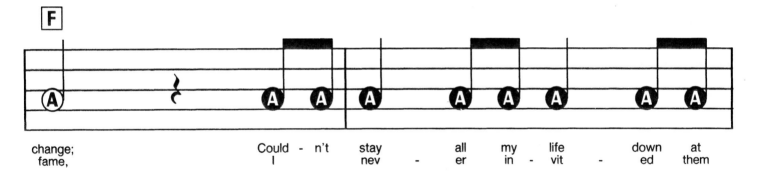

change; Could - n't stay all my life down at
fame, I nev - er in - vit - ed them

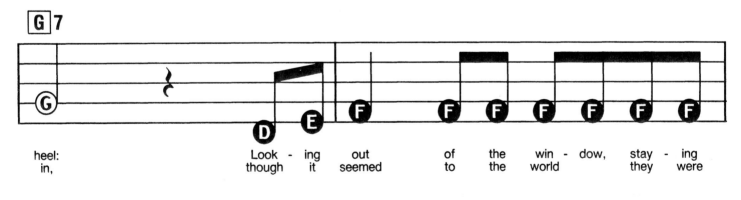

heel: Look - ing out of the win - dow, stay - ing
in, though it seemed to the world they were

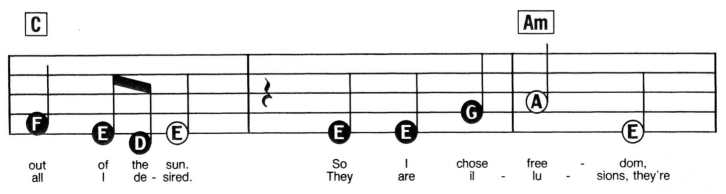

out of the sun. So I chose free - dom,
all I de - sired. They are il - lu - sions, they're

20

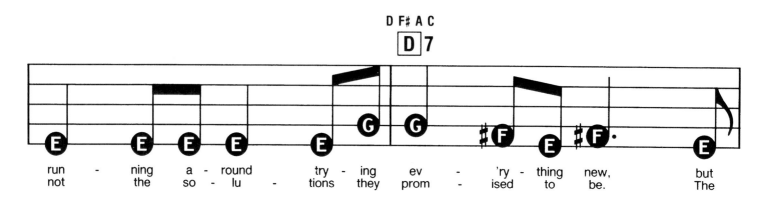

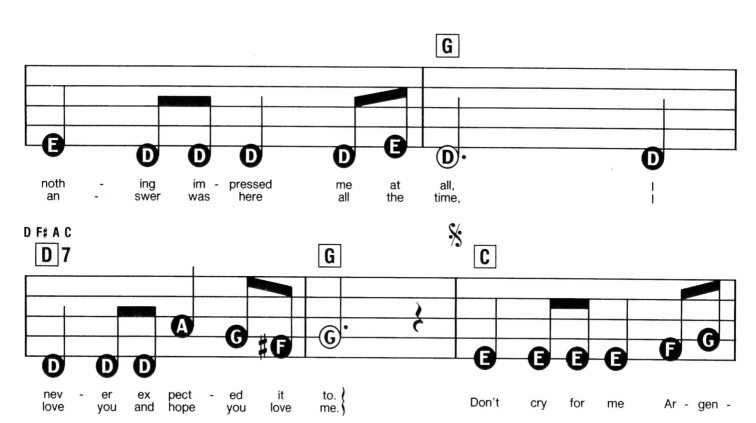

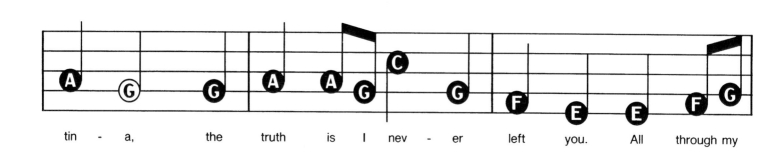

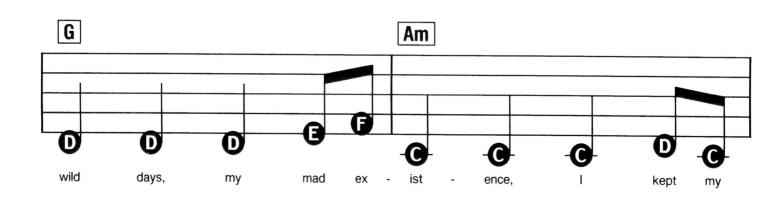

21

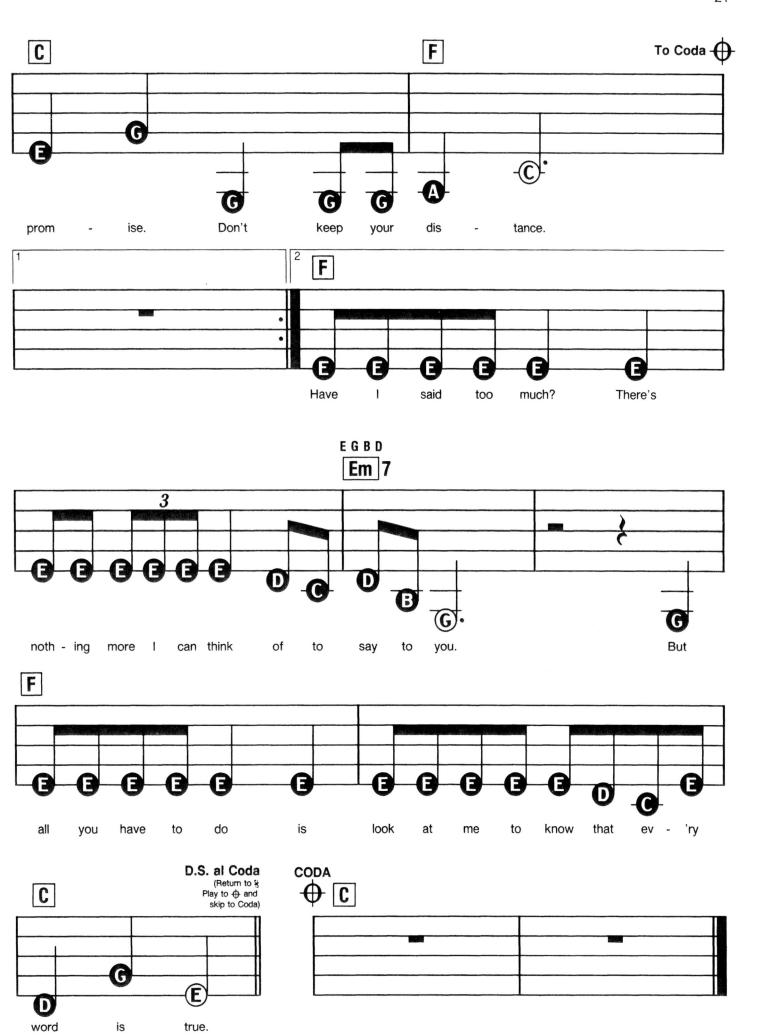

HOW SONGS ARE BUILT

It's not necessary or even desirable to play double notes throughout an entire song. But how do you decide where to change playing styles? Knowing something about music **form** will be helpful.

As the words in this book form sentences, and the sentences form paragraphs, music has a similar structure. Groups of notes form **fragments** of various lengths. For example, the three notes that match the words "Jingle Bells" are a fragment; this fragment repeats. "Jingle all the way" is another fragment. Together, these make a **phrase**. When a number of phrases are combined, they make a **section**, or **strain**. A section might be called a **verse** ("Dashing through the snow..."), or a **chorus** ("Jingle bells, Jingle bells..."). On a larger scale, a symphony or a concerto consists of **movements**, which are made up of many sections.

Before you play a song, look over the music and determine where the various parts begin. To keep things interesting, play some phrases or sections with double notes and others without.

INDEPENDENT DOUBLE NOTES

The opposite of parallel double notes is independent double notes. Instead of following the movement of the melody, these move on their own. The following material introduces situations that occur in almost every song you play. Independent double notes aid these situations and make playing double notes easier, as well as adding interest and variety to your playing.

STRONG LINES

In many songs, some of the accompaniment chords include a tone that tends to move very strongly to a particular note in a following chord. Most often this movement is in half steps, e.g. E to F to F♯. The line may progress up or down the staff.

Such movement, which we call "strong lines," makes a great source of double notes. Here are the chords from the opening measures of your next song, CLIMB EV'RY MOUNTAIN.

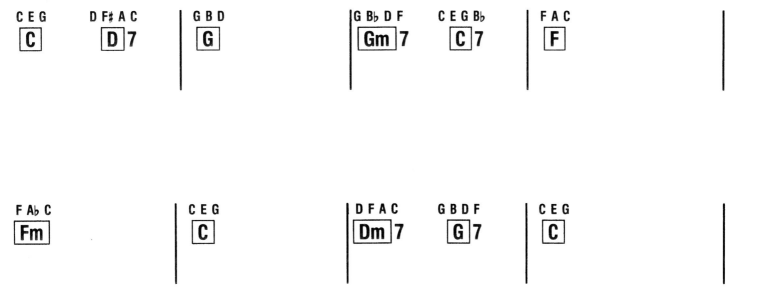

If you use C as the first double note (below the melody note E) in the song, you can locate a strong line that is eight measures long. Try it, starting on C and circling the note in each chord that you think should be used (Hint: the double notes will all be whole notes).

Here are the results written out on the staff.

If you take the time to look over the music of a song you wish to play, you'll likely be able to find similar strong lines and use them to benefit your playing.

This selection from *The Sound of Music* introduces you to one of the many song forms in popular music: the A-A-B-A form.

The first eight measures, with which you're already familiar, form the first section (called "A"). The next eight measures are similar enough that they are collectively called "A" as well. The next eight measures (starting where the two eighth notes first appear) are entirely different; therefore, this section is called "B." Musicians call it "the bridge." The final eight measures start with a return to the melody of the opening of the song, hence this section is also called "A." But wait — the melody starts in a different place! The composer probably wanted a "lift" in the music here, to reflect the inspirational lyrics. Nevertheless, the section is still called "A."

The sections are marked for your convenience to help you know logical places to change double note styles. Sometimes changing styles is a matter of choice; other times it's a necessity.

Here's the entire arrangement of CLIMB EV'RY MOUNTAIN. Notice that there's a strong line moving up in measure 31. Once you can play the arrangement, see how much of the song works with parallel double notes. Maybe your own arrangement will use both independent and parallel double notes.

Climb Ev'ry Mountain

(From "THE SOUND OF MUSIC")

Registration 2
Rhythm: March or Swing

Lyrics by Oscar Hammerstein II
Music by Richard Rodgers

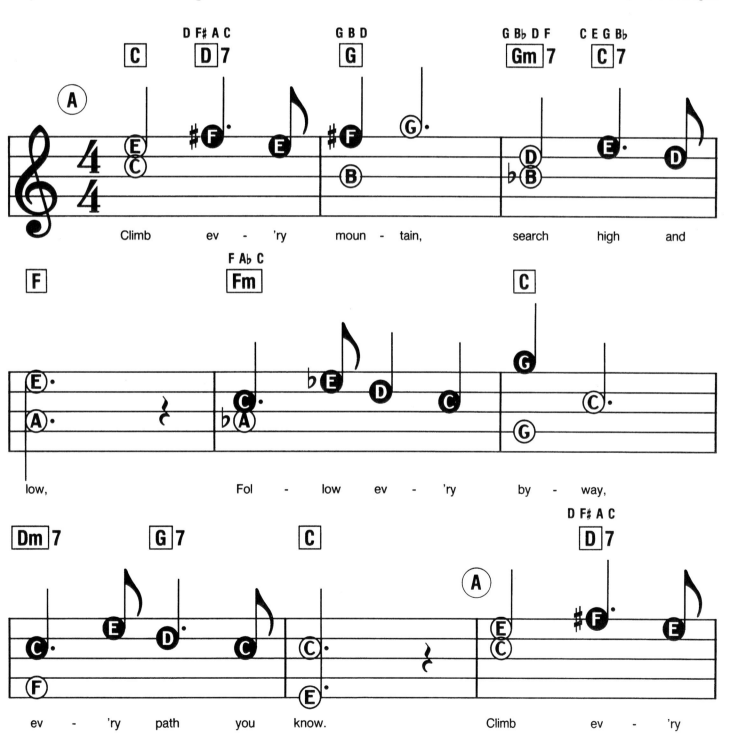

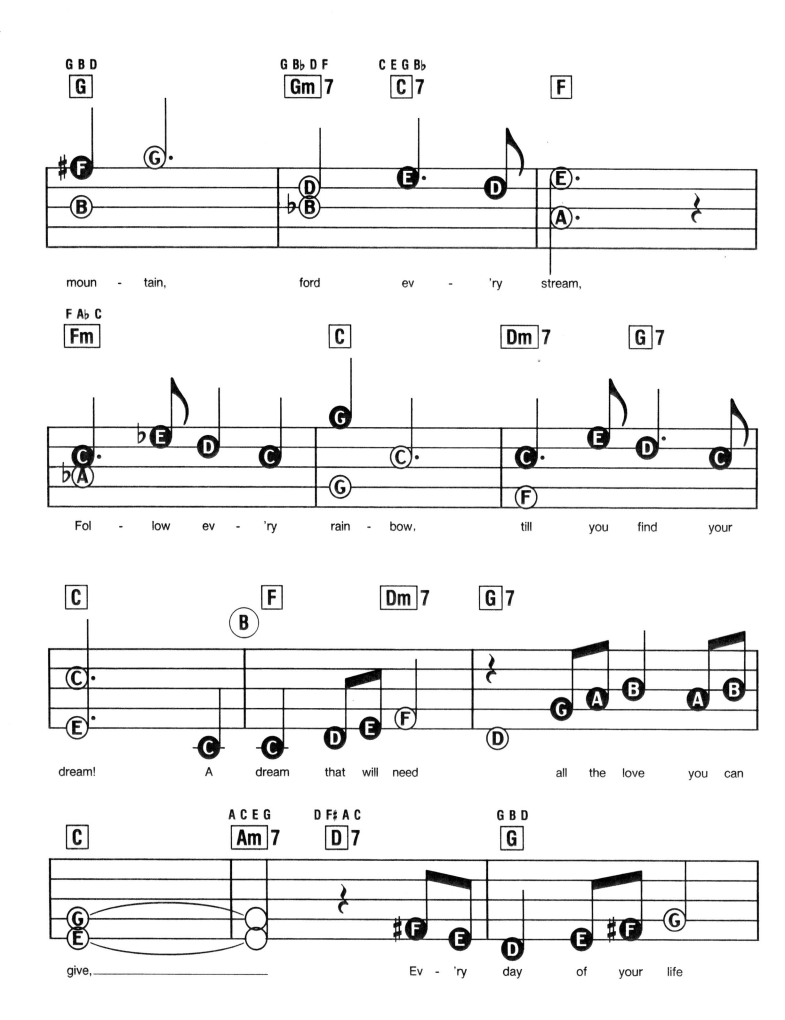

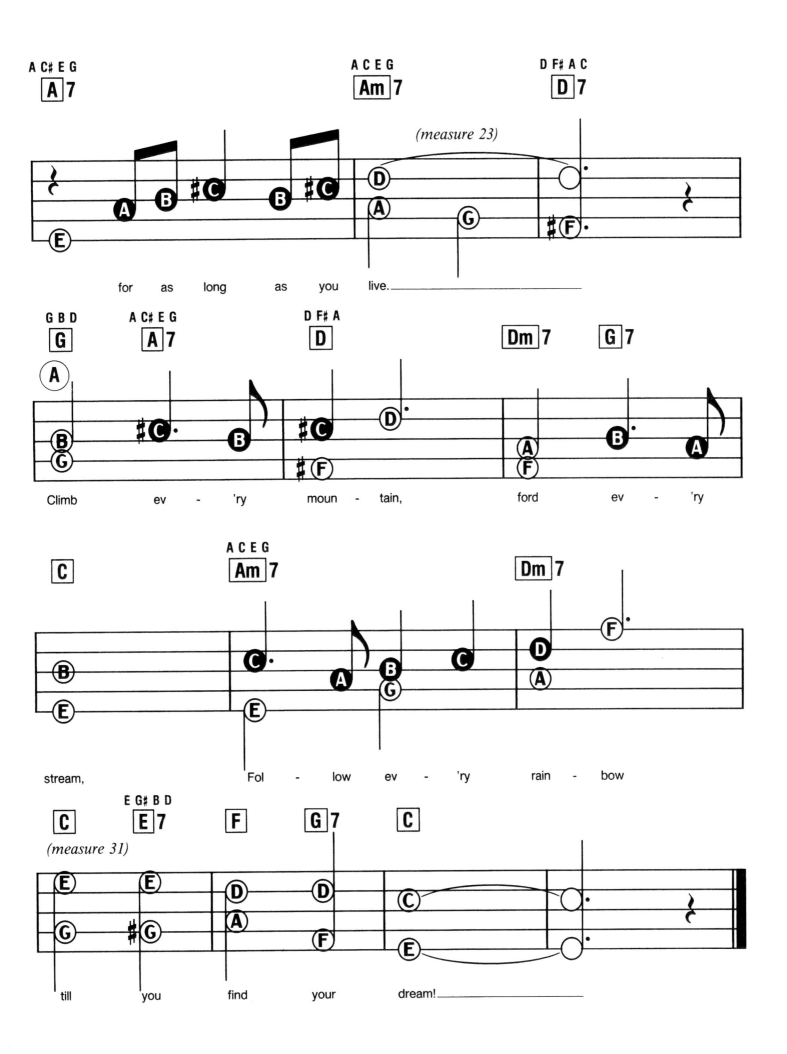

MELODY HOLDS, HARMONY MOVES

In measures 23 and 24 of CLIMB EV'RY MOUNTAIN, the melody note is seven beats long and the double notes are in half notes, A to G to F♯, forming a strong line. Almost every song has places where the melody "pauses" rhythmically, by holding on a longer note. This occurs most often at the end of a phrase or between sections. You can add interest and a professional touch to your arrangement by using independent double notes to fill in such places.

When you choose to use this technique, it's often helpful to look for notes in the accompaniment chords that create strong-line movement, as we did in the last song. Other times, chord tones can be used, either alone or connected by non-chord passing tones.

Two possibilities are demonstrated in MARIANNE: Stepwise movement using chord tones and some passing non-chord tones, and an "echo" effect where the double notes "answer" the melody. Each occurrence is marked.

C E G   G B D F
C   **G** 7

Marianne

Registration 2
Rhythm: 16 Beat or Disco

All   day,   all   night,   Mar - i - anne,_____ *——stepwise——*

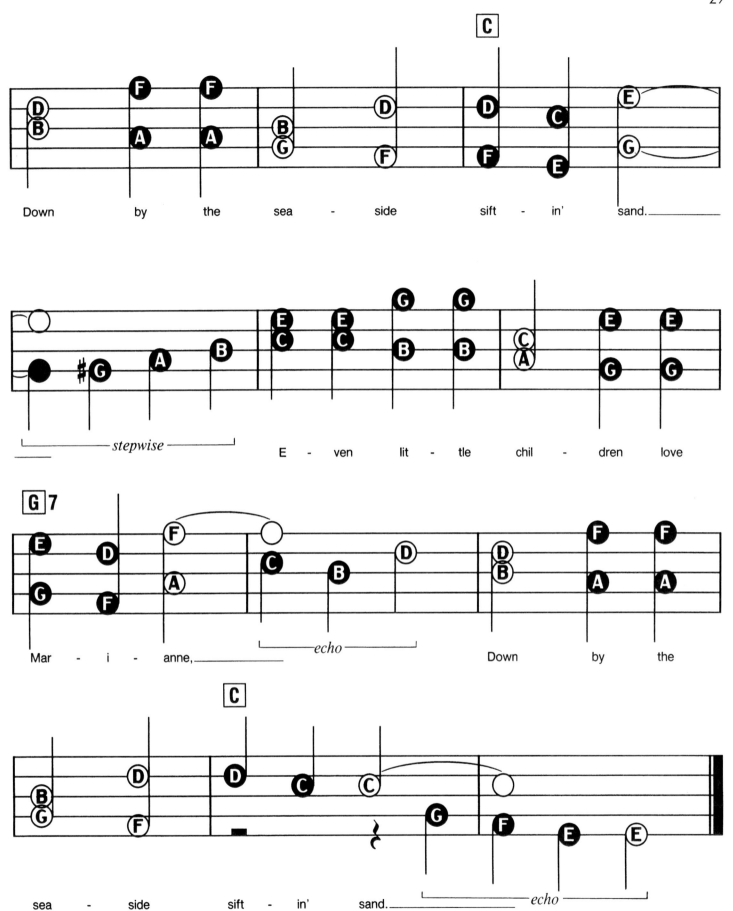

Spend some time on this song, working out your own ideas for fill-ins using double notes. Also look for such opportunities in the next song, CRAZY, and the remaining songs in this book.

Crazy

Registration 2
Rhythm: Country or Swing

Words and Music by
Willie Nelson

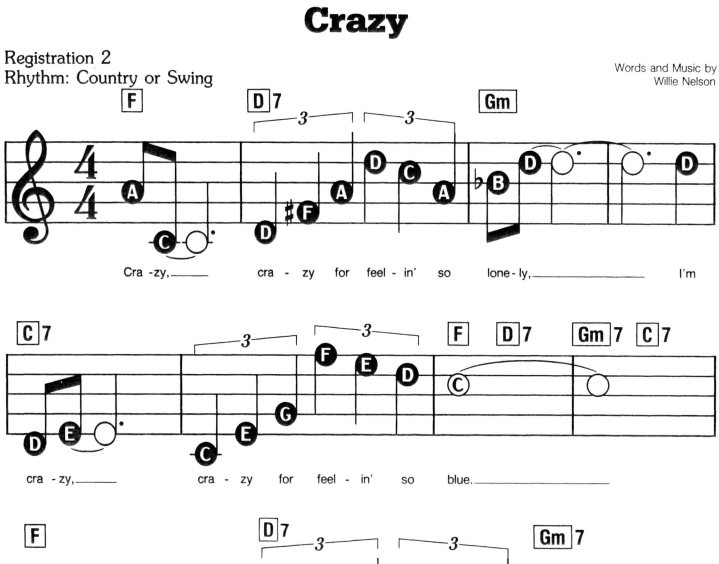

Cra-zy,_____ cra-zy for feel-in' so lone-ly,_____ I'm

cra-zy,_____ cra-zy for feel-in' so blue._____

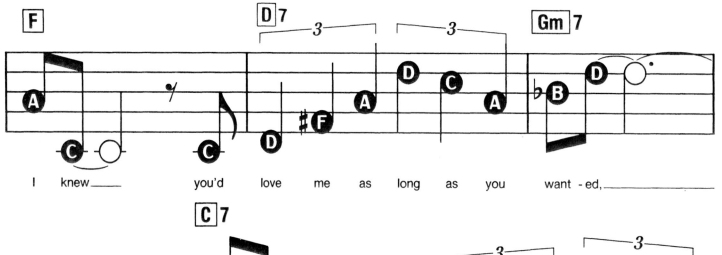

I knew_____ you'd love me as long as you want-ed,_____

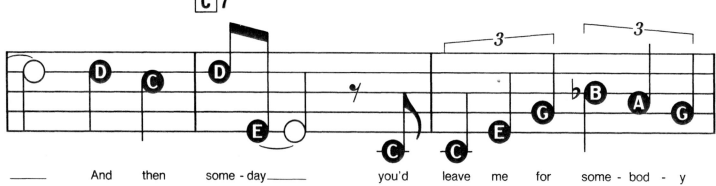

_____ And then some-day_____ you'd leave me for some-bod-y

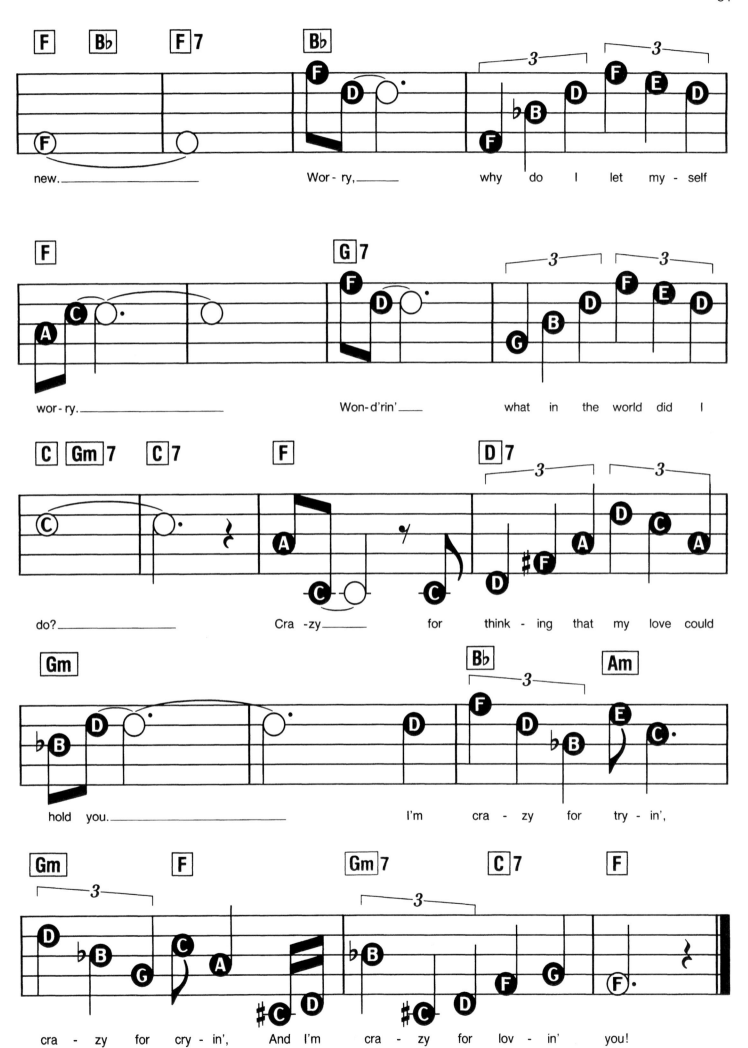

MELODY MOVES, HARMONY HOLDS

Where the melody moves rather quickly (shorter notes), or the tempo (playing speed of the song) is a bit fast, longer harmony notes smooth out the sound and make the song easier to play.

The following examples are from CALL ME, a hit from the bossa nova craze in the '60s. Study and play each of them. Notice in the first one that the intervals created by the long notes in the strong line all sound good because each happens quickly and is gone. Notice also that the long notes are all chord tones. Use a sustaining voice like a flute or clarinet so the double notes sound as long as you hold down the key.

Call Me

Words and Music by
Tony Hatch

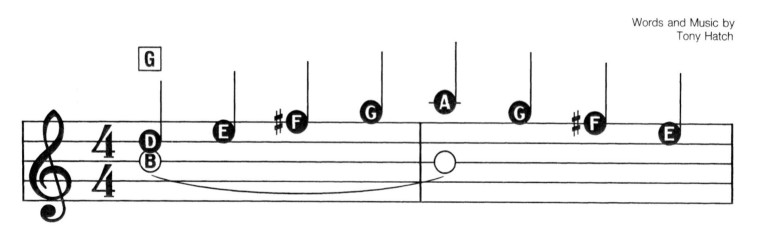

The next example shows that you need not use double notes in every measure.

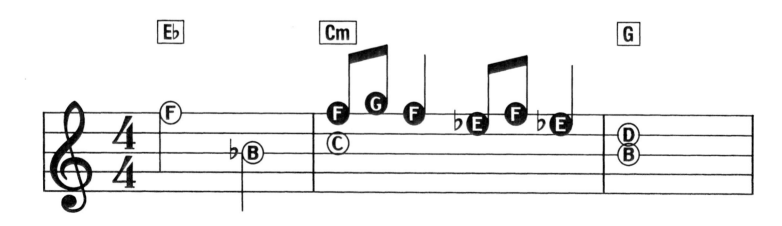

Play the entire arrangement of CALL ME and listen to the effect of the independent double notes. Then apply what you've learned to JUST BECAUSE on page 36.

ACE **Am** ACEG **Am**7 B♭DFA♭ **B♭**7 CEGB♭ **C**7 CE♭G **Cm** DF#AC **D**7 E♭GB♭ **E♭** FAC **F** FA♭C **Fm** GBD **G** GB♭D **Gm**

Call Me

Registration 3
Rhythm: Bossa Nova or Latin

Words and Music by
Tony Hatch

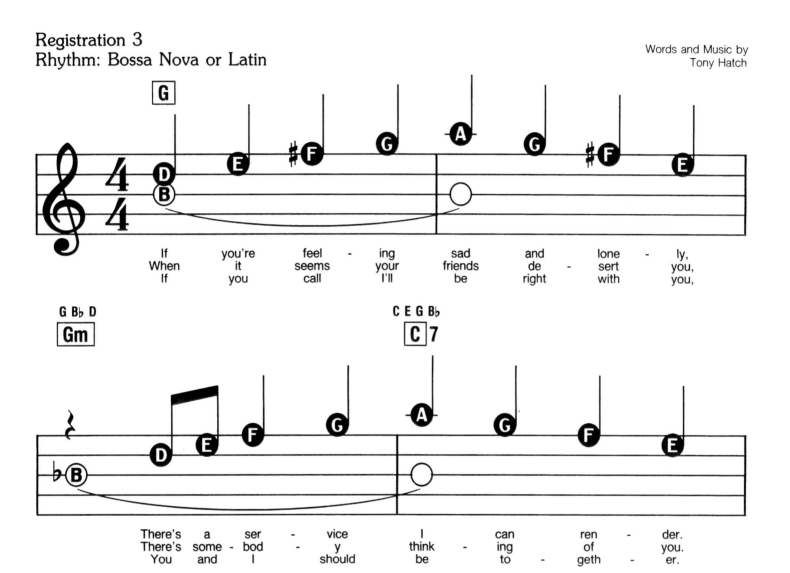

If you're feel - ing sad and lone - ly,
When it seems your friends de - sert you,
If you call I'll be right with you,

There's a ser - vice I can ren - der.
There's some - bod - y think - ing of you.
You and I should be to - geth - er.

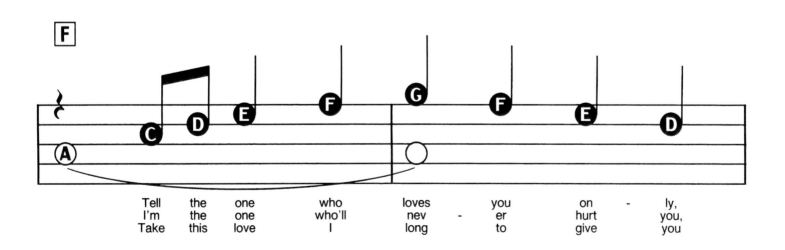

Tell the one who loves you on - ly,
I'm the one who'll nev - er hurt you,
Take this love long to give you

MCA MUSIC PUBLISHING

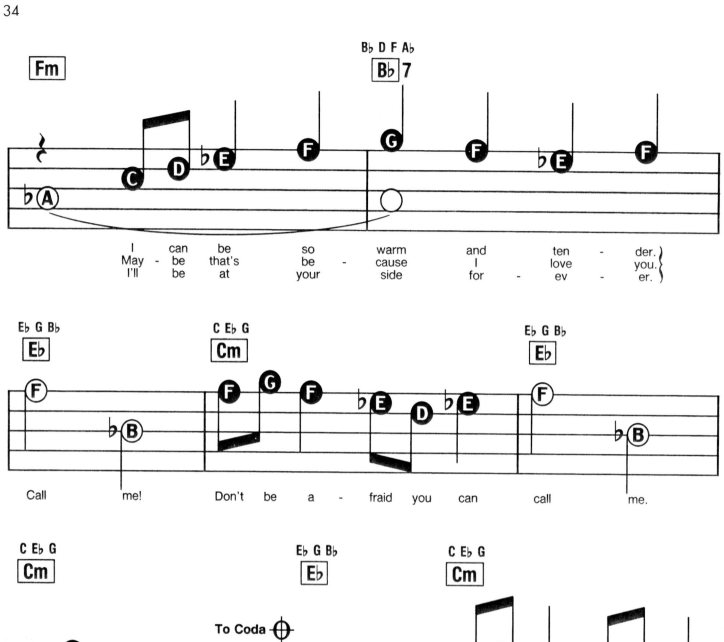

I can be so warm and ten - der.
May - be that's so be - cause I love you.
I'll be at your side for - ev - er.

Call me! Don't be a - fraid you can call me.

May - be it's late but just call me! Tell me and I'll be a -

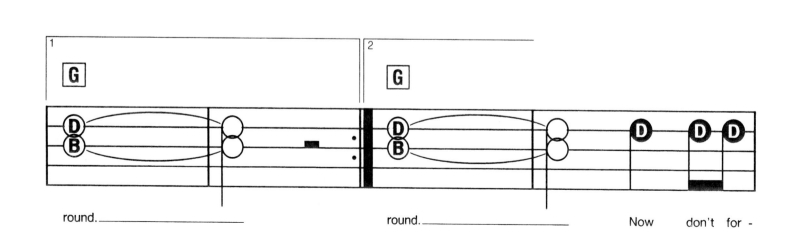

round._____ round._____ Now don't for -

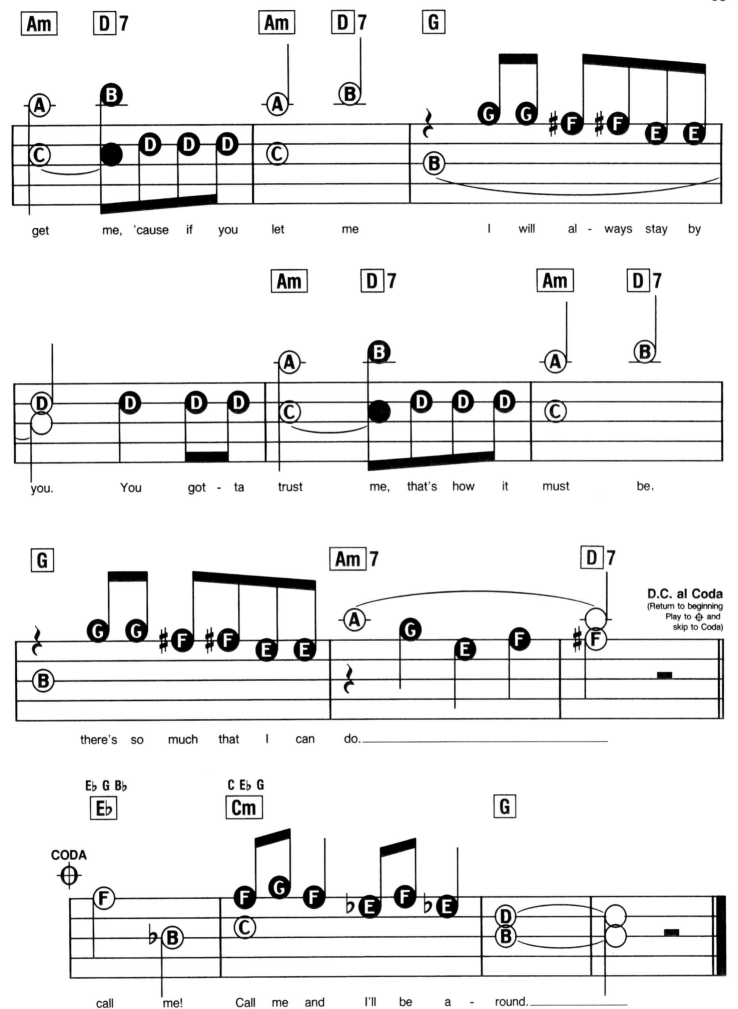

A C♯ E G C E G D F♯ A C F A C F A♭ C G B D F

A7 C D7 F Fm G7

Just Because

Registration 5
Rhythm: Polka or March

Words and Music by
Bob and Joe Shelton and Sid Robin

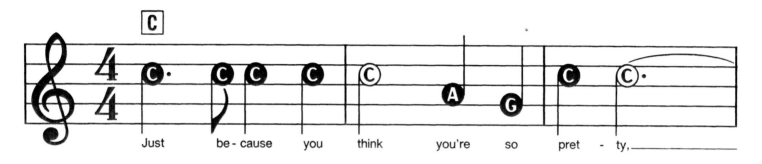

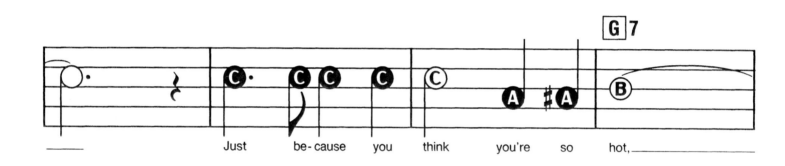

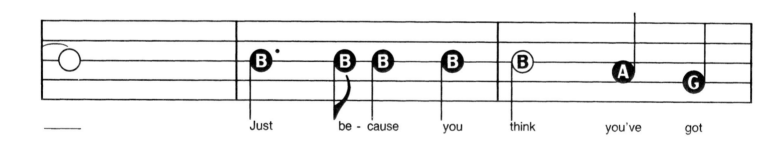

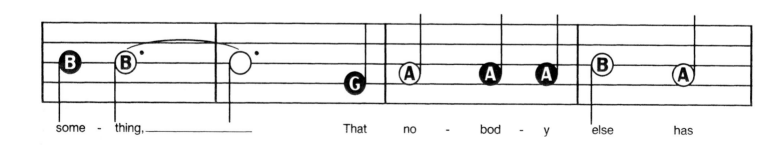

37

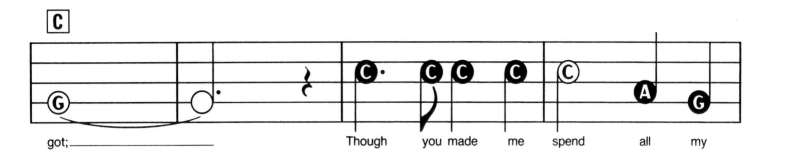

got;_____ Though you made me spend all my

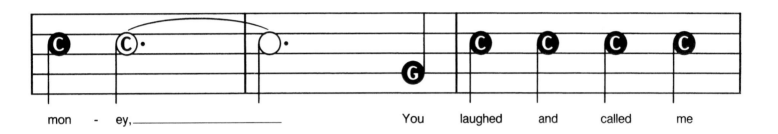

mon - ey,_____ You laughed and called me

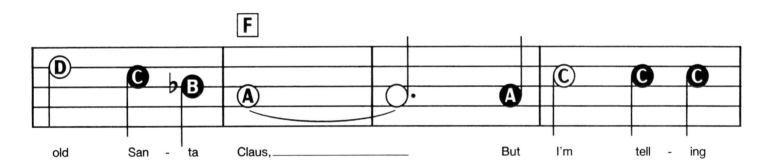

old San - ta Claus,_____ But I'm tell - ing

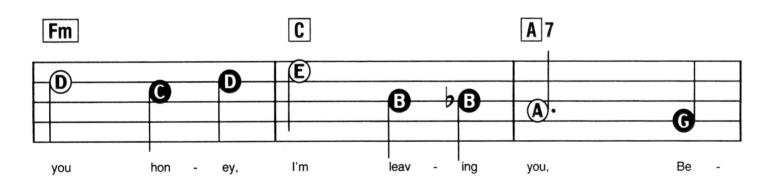

you hon - ey, I'm leav - ing you, Be -

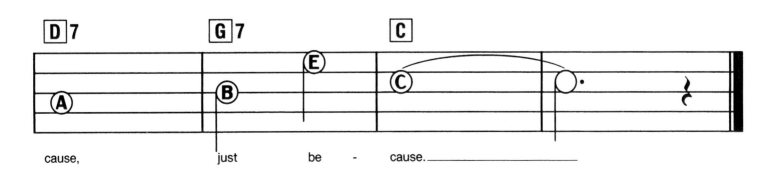

cause, just be - cause._____

LEAPS IN THE MELODY

Certain parts of some songs seem difficult to harmonize because of leaps in the melody. THE ENTERTAINER is an example of this. The example below shows how the leaps can be harmonized using the guidelines you've learned thus far.

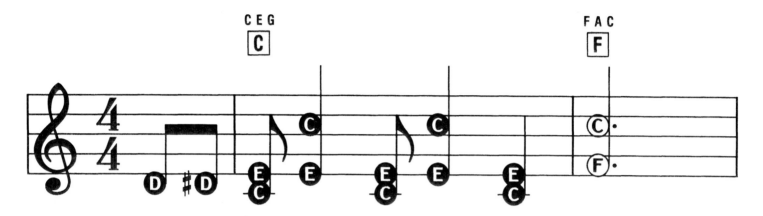

While it is correct, it's also awkward and difficult to play. Here's a solution.

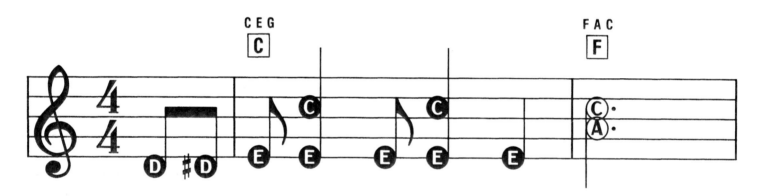

The idea is to leave out some of the double notes, making the leaps easier to play while maintaining the double note style.

Here's THE ENTERTAINER, showing how the leaps and the eighth-note fragments can be harmonized. Try the right hand part alone before you add the chords.

The Entertainer

Registration 8
Rhythm: March or Swing

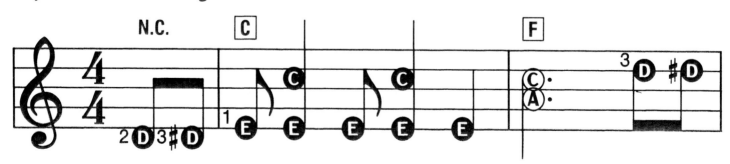

39

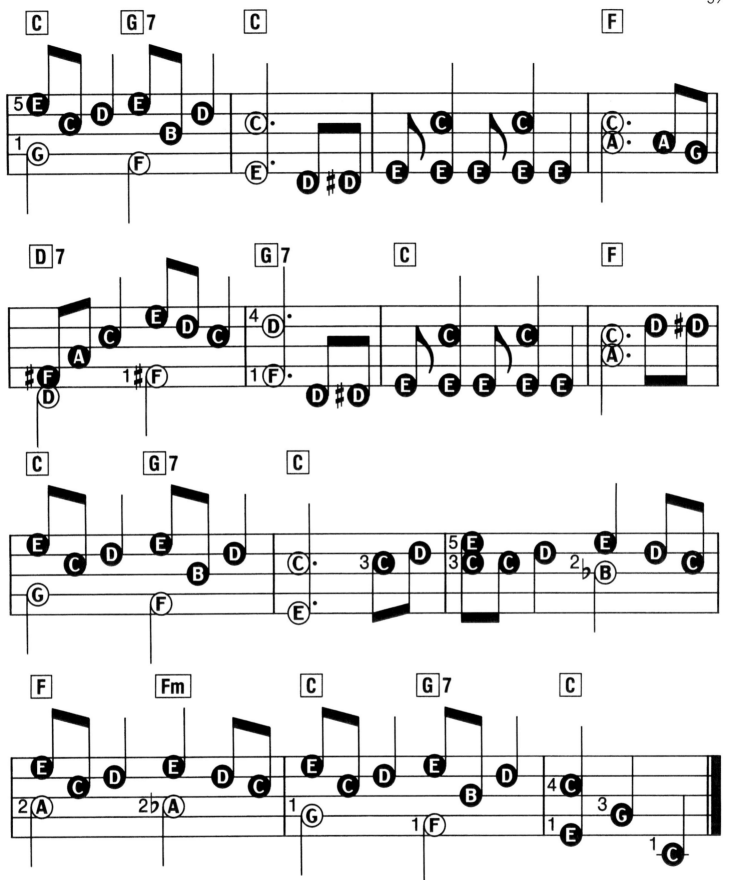

The final song gives you the chance to review everything you've learned by applying the various double note styles. More than one technique will work in most places so take your time — and have fun!

Somewhere Out There
(From "AN AMERICAN TAIL")

Registration 4
Rhythm: Rock or 8 Beat

By James Horner,
Barry Mann and Cynthia Weil

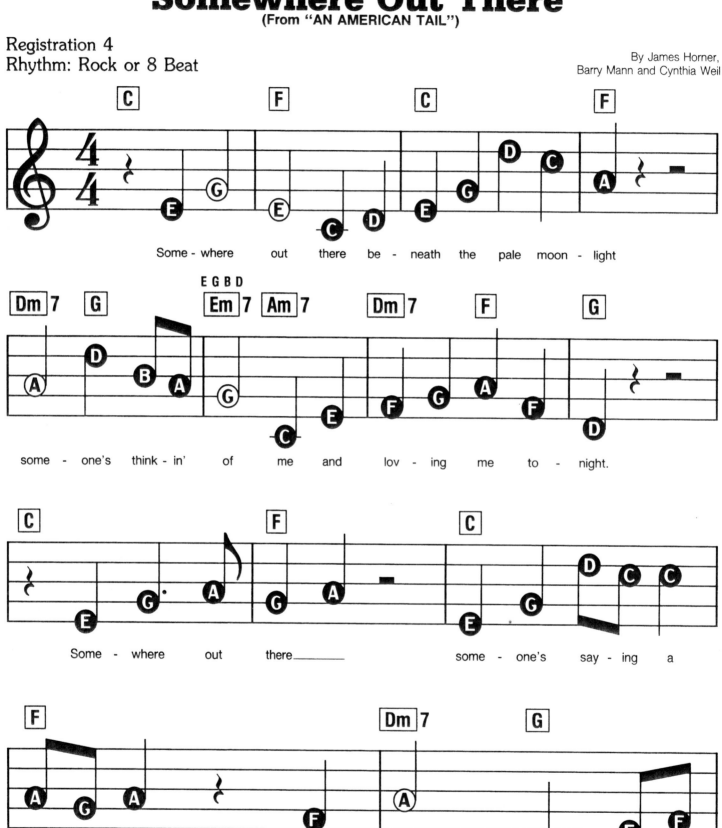

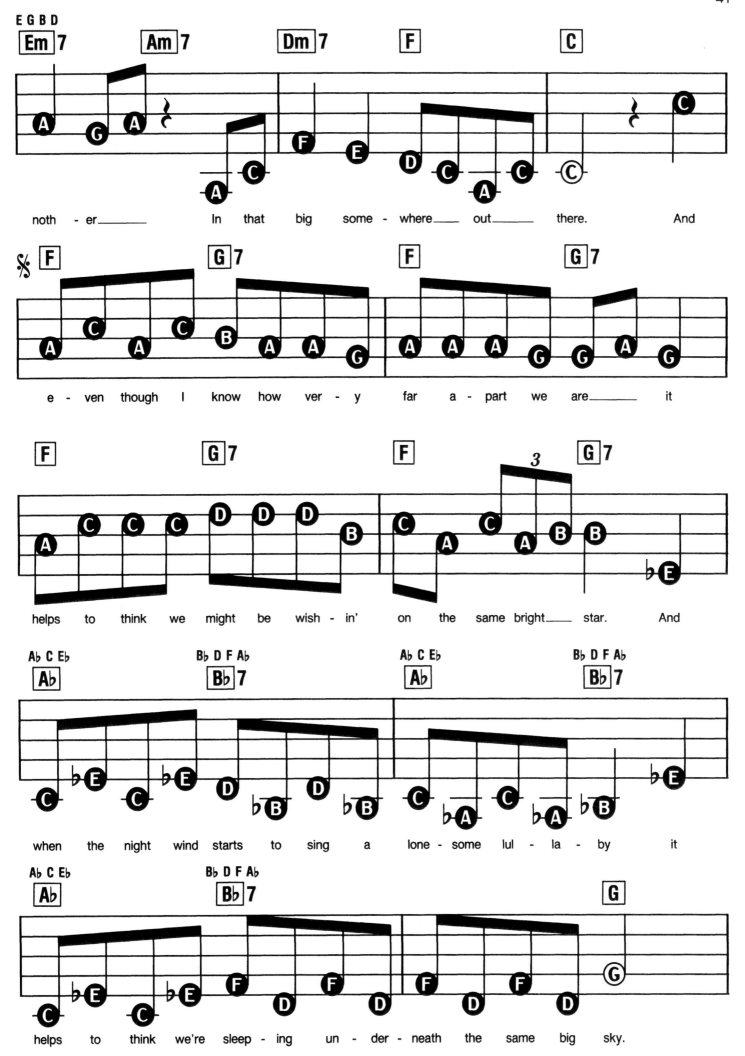

42

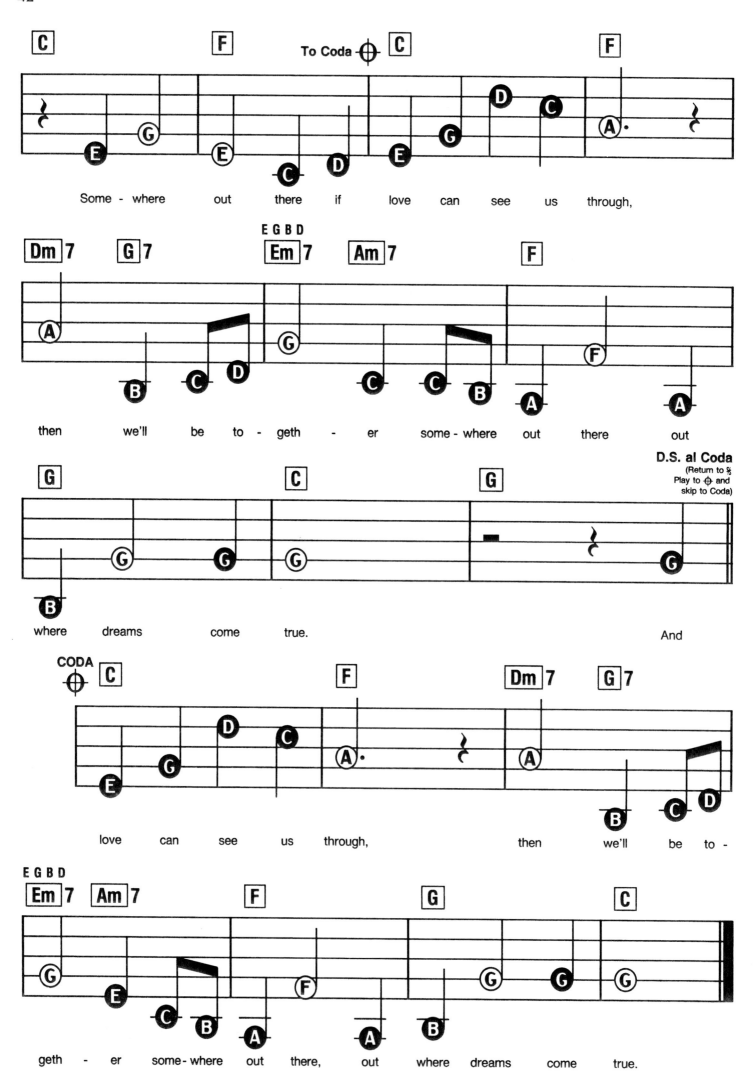

MUSIC BASICS

Notation

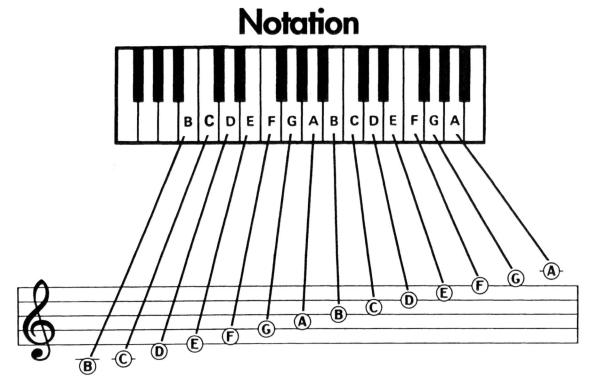

Sharps And Flats

A SHARP (♯) in front of a note raises the pitch of the note a half step, or to the adjacent key to the right.

A FLAT (♭) in front of a note lowers the pitch of the note a half step, or to the adjacent key to the left.

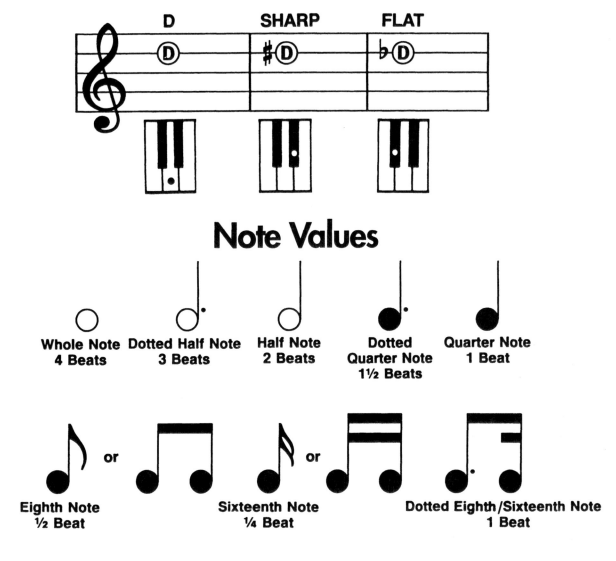

Note Values

Whole Note
4 Beats

Dotted Half Note
3 Beats

Half Note
2 Beats

Dotted Quarter Note
1½ Beats

Quarter Note
1 Beat

Eighth Note
½ Beat
or

Sixteenth Note
¼ Beat
or

Dotted Eighth/Sixteenth Note
1 Beat

Rests

▬	▬	𝄽	𝄾	𝄿
Whole Rest **4 Beats**	**Half Rest** **2 Beats**	**Quarter Rest** **1 Beat**	**Eighth Rest** **½ Beat**	**Sixteenth Rest** **¼ Beat**

Bar Lines and Measures

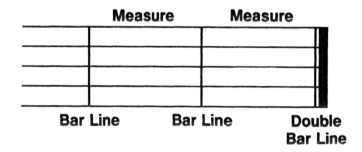

Measure   Measure

Bar Line   Bar Line   Double
Bar Line

Time Signatures

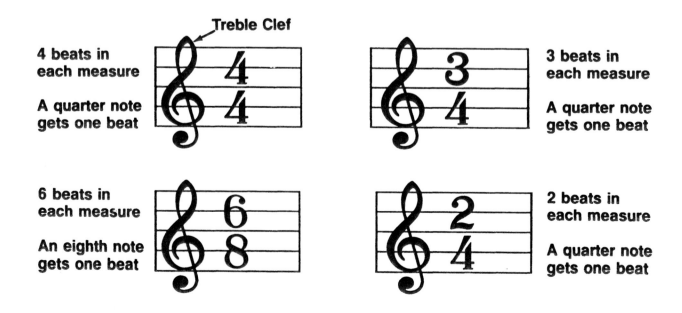

Treble Clef

4 beats in
each measure

A quarter note
gets one beat

3 beats in
each measure

A quarter note
gets one beat

6 beats in
each measure

An eighth note
gets one beat

2 beats in
each measure

A quarter note
gets one beat

Ties

A TIE is a curved line that connects two consecutive notes with the same note name and pitch. When a TIE appears in the music, play the first note and then continue to hold the note down through the full value of the second note.

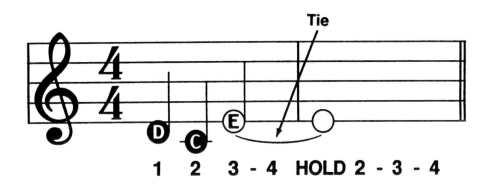

Pickup Notes

Sometimes the first measure will have an incomplete number of beats. These notes are called PICKUP NOTES. The last measure in the song provides the missing beats.

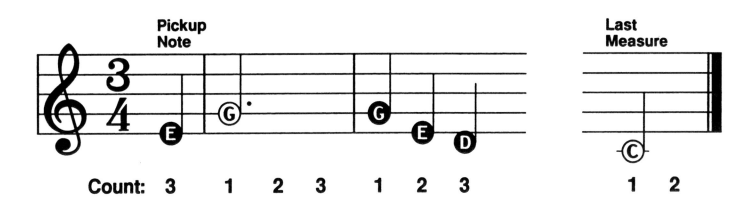

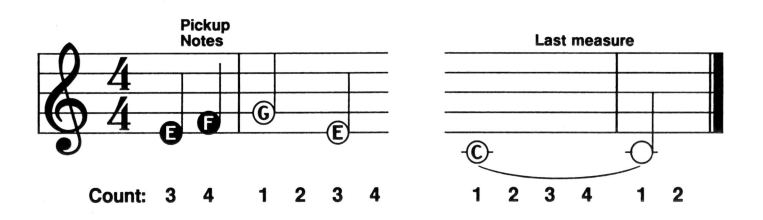

Repeat Sign

Repeat Signs are used in a song when a section of the arrangement or the entire song is to be played again (repeated). Generally, Repeat Signs appear in sets of two.

- There will be one repeat sign (A) at the beginning of the section to be repeated.

- Play up to the repeat sign at the end of the section (B).

- Return to the first repeat sign (A) and play the section again.

- If there is no repeat sign (A), return to the beginning of the song.

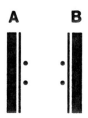

1st And 2nd Endings

When two different endings appear within or at the end of a song, here's what to do:

- Play the song up through the first (1) ending.

- Repeat to the closest repeat sign, or back to the beginning.

- Play that section again, skip the first ending (1), but play the second ending (2).

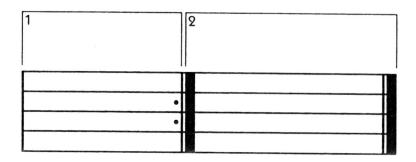

Triplet

A "triplet" is a group of three notes played in the same amount of time as two notes of the same time value. A triplet is indicated by the number 3 above or below the notes.

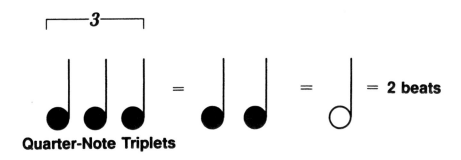

Quarter-Note Triplets

Eighth-Note Triplets

Terms

D.S. al Coda – Return to 𝄋, play up to "To Coda," skip to "Coda" section.

D.S. al Fine – Return to 𝄋, play up through Fine (end of song).

D.C. al Coda – Return to the beginning and play to this sign ⊕. Then skip to the section marked "Coda."

Repeat and Fade – Repeat to beginning or to last repeat sign, and gradually fade out by decreasing volume.

Registration Guide

- Match the Registration number on the song to the corresponding numbered category below. Select and activate an instrumental sound available on your instrument.

- Choose an automatic rhythm appropriate to the mood and style of the song. (Consult your Owner's Guide for proper operation of automatic rhythm features.)

- Adjust the tempo and volume controls to comfortable settings.

Registration

1	Flutes, Clarinet, Oboe, Flugel Horn, Trombone, French Horn, Organ Flutes
2	Saxophones, Trumpet, Mute Trumpet, Synth Leads, Jazz/Gospel Organs
3	Acoustic/Electric Guitars, Banjo, Mandolin, Dulcimer, Ukulele, Hawaiian Guitar
4	Violin, Viola, Cello, Fiddle, String Ensemble, Pizzicato, Organ Strings
5	Vibraphone, Marimba, Xylophone, Steel Drums, Bells, Celesta, Chimes
6	Accordion, French Accordion, Mussette, Harmonica, Pump Organ, Bagpipes
7	Pipe Organ, Hand Bells, Vocal Ensemble, Choir, Organ Flutes
8	Piano, Electric Piano, Honky Tonk Piano, Harpsichord, Clavi
9	Melodic Percussion, Wah Trumpet, Synth, Whistle, Kazoo, Perc. Organ
10	Bass Section, Sax Section, Wind Ensemble, Full Organ, Theater Organ